Affiliate Marketing for Beginners

Launching your first internet business the easy way.

IQ PRESS, INC.

Disclaimer

The Publisher has strived to be as accurate and complete as possible in the creation of this report, notwithstanding the fact that it does not warrant or represent at any time that the contents within are accurate due to the rapidly changing nature of the Internet.

The Publisher will not be responsible for any losses or damages of any kind incurred by the reader whether directly or indirectly arising from the use of the information found in this report.

This report is not intended for use as a source of legal, business, accounting or financial advice. All readers are advised to seek services of competent professionals in legal, business, accounting, and finance field.

No guarantees of income are made. Reader assumes responsibility for use of information contained herein. The author reserves the right to make changes without notice. The Publisher assumes no responsibility or liability whatsoever on the behalf of the reader of this report.

CONTENTS

ACKNOWLEDGMENTS

IQ Press, Inc. is a small publishing company dedicated to providing access to educational materials primarily in small business start-up and development. Their mission is to bring the reader useful information that can be implemented with a small capital outlay and generate income streams for the reader to implement.

We hope you enjoy these reports and that they will help improve your life.

www.IQPress.org

Chapter 1: What to expect as an Affiliate Marketer – The Lifestyle

If you're looking to make a ton of money online, then the best option for most people is undoubtedly affiliate marketing. This is the online business model with the lowest barriers to entry that anyone can learn and master. At the same time, it is potentially one of the most profitable business models you can use online and certainly much more profitable than blogging for AdSense revenue or similar schemes.

This is a point that advertisers on Facebook often like to labor. Chances are that you have seen plenty of adverts for online money making schemes and 'programs'. No doubt, 9 out of 10 times, they'll be based around affiliate marketing.

You'll know these ads when you see them. They're the ones where people talk to you from their private yacht and tell you how they make a 6-figure salary in just a few hours of work each week.

Likewise, you have probably seen the videos of online 'billionaires' talking about their money-making systems while wearing smart suits in very pimped-out offices. They've created a 'digital empire' all their own using affiliate marketing techniques and now they're rich and powerful and you probably want to be them… But is any of this true?

Can you really accomplish all that through affiliate marketing?

Is it really that easy?

Or is there more to it than that?

How Much Can an Affiliate Marketer Make?

First of all, let's assess the claims about earnings. During the Affiliate Summit over 1,800 affiliate marketers completed a survey describing everything from their methods to their earnings.

How much were they bringing in?

Well, only 46% earned less than $20K while 8% earned $50K-$100K and 12% earned $100K+. At the very least, this shows it's certainly very possible to earn big money. (The rest were around the middle, but note that 19% elected not to answer at all.)

What's also interesting here is the sheer spread of earnings. Affiliate marketing is bringing in from $20K to $100K and beyond, which you just don't find in traditional careers.

So what's making the big difference?

It's the skill of the individual.

As an affiliate marketer, you're self-employed and working alone. There's no need to 'climb the corporate ladder' or to compete for promotions. You can get to the top overnight if you have the right skills because it's all up to you.

In this book, we'll be looking at the secrets you need to really start earning the big bucks as an affiliate marketer.

The Affiliate Marketing Lifestyle: What Does Affiliate Marketing Involve?

Perhaps the biggest draw of affiliate marketing is not just the money. Instead, for many people, the appeal lies in the fact that this is a completely 'passive' business model. Once you've set everything up, such as your sales funnel, your affiliate network account and your blog/sales page, then you can literally be earning money while you're sleeping or away on holiday.

But again this can get twisted. This lifestyle is what you can achieve once you're at the top of your game as an affiliate marketer – it doesn't come overnight.
In fact, affiliate marketing is likely to initially involve a lot of work. The idea here is that you put in the work up front so that you can sow the seeds of your labor further down the line. To begin with, you need to be willing to put in a lot of hours for very little reward.

Specifically then, what does affiliate marketing involve?

If you're reading this book, then there's a good chance you have a general idea but we'll recap in a little more detail for those who do not.

Essentially, as an affiliate marketer, you sell products for commission. This means you'll be finding products online and promoting them using your own affiliate link. If someone clicks on your link and then buys the product, you'll get a cut of the profit. Often, affiliate marketing involves selling digital products and you can expect your cut to be as much as 50% all the way up to 75% of the sales price.

There's no risk involved for you because you're not creating the product and there's nothing for you to ship or to store. All you have to do is sell, but you can earn more than the creator.

The hard part, though is in doing that selling. This is where the 'marketing' part comes in and your job is to find yourself a large audience - through a blog, through an e-mail campaign, through advertising or through social media - whatever tool you find the most effective.

This is why there's no steep learning curve or barrier for entry for beginners. All you're literally doing is making sure people see your affiliate link. There's no product creation and no investment. You can get started tomorrow in minutes and it won't cost you a penny.

If you're a big blogger and you already have an audience of 10,000 readers a day then you're going to find this very easy. All you have to do is put some very persuasive text on your website along with the link and you'll start driving traffic. If this is your first attempt at affiliate marketing though, then you may well find this process a little more complex and little more difficult.

You now have two options:

Build your own audience
Advertise

(Actually, there are other methods and growth hacks you can use which we'll come to later, but for now this will suffice.)

Advertising

If you're going the route of paid advertising, then that means you're likely going to be using PPC. This is 'Pay-Per-Click' and basically means that you pay for every person who clicks on an ad and thus gets sent to your site. The more you pay, the more visitors you get.

If you design your site well and you can really convince people to buy your products, then you should be able to convert a predictable amount of visitors into buyers. This in turn means you can work out your precise ROI. So if you pay a certain amount per visitor, and N percentage of those visitors earn you X amount of money, you can tell whether or not your strategy is profitable.

The amount you pay per click will depend on the amount of competition available for your ad. PPC ads work on a 'bidding' system, whereby the advertiser offering the most per click is the advertiser whose ad is most likely to show.

Meanwhile, even if your website is very effective at convincing people to buy, you'll still only get 0.5%-10% of visitors converting (and more often, you'll be at the bottom end of that spectrum). So you'll need your ad to be seen by about 10-200 people in order for you to get a single sale, which means you may be paying a relatively high amount for your ad to be seen 10,000 to 20,000 times for about 100 sales.

This is a formula that takes a lot of adjusting and you can expect to lose a certain amount of money before you get it right. With a good set-up, you can expect to spend $600 a day on PPC to make about $200 profit. That's quite a big risk when you're first starting out and for the first few months you probably will be operating at a loss (until you learn the right keywords to target, the right products to sell, the right sales pitch etc.). The information in this book should help you minimize the time it takes to become profitable.

Building an Audience

If you don't have that kind of money to play around with, then your only other option is to build your audience naturally over time.

That means creating a blog and then using it to promote yourself through social media to build up a mailing list of subscribers. Again, you can't expect your conversion rate to be all that high and you're going to need about 10,000 views daily to make even close to a full time living.

Getting to this point is slow going. You can expect it to take at least a year before you're on 600 visitors a day and while you'll accumulate exponential growth at this point, it will still likely be a few years before you're at 10,000.

Oh and at this point, affiliate marketing is anything but passive. At this stage, you'll be investing huge amounts of time into writing a compelling blog that people will want to follow, emailing your subscribers and managing advertising campaigns.

It is very possible to be highly successful at affiliate marketing. You definitely can earn hundreds of thousands from it and once you're all set up, the money will come in while you sleep.

But it also requires a big upfront investment of time and/or money, along with the right know-how and strategy. If it didn't, then everyone would be rich, no one would work for an employer and the economy would have collapsed.

So it's a good thing really…

How to Approach Affiliate Marketing

That last paragraph wasn't intended to depress you and hopefully you haven't put the book/tablet down and abandoned all hope at this point. This is simply a reality check.

What it means, is that you need to set out with not only the right attitude, but also the right expectations. Don't go into affiliate marketing thinking you'll be a millionaire overnight because you'll only be sorely disappointed; and this will lead to you giving up. Instead, understand that this is a process and that to begin with, it's not going to be your sole income.

The way you get around this is to make affiliate marketing into a kind of hobby on top of your regular job. This might seem like a lot of work but if you can find the time in the evening to upload three articles per week and do a little bit of marketing, you should be able to make some steady progress. If you can invest 3 hours a week, this is likely enough.

While you won't be rich, the rewards for this will still be impressive.

Let's say you start making one sale a week at $40 profit. You're not paying for advertising but rather building your blog organically.

This now means you're making an additional $160 a month. That in turn is an impressive $1,920 annually on top of your regular salary. In other words, it's easily enough to enjoy a free holiday, or to buy yourself a nice computer and some new clothes.

This will accelerate pretty fast, earning you $5,000 or $10,000 over the year. Even if you never progress beyond that point, you've now massively increased your annual salary and you can now think about living a completely different lifestyle.

You'll have financial security, a backup in case you ever find yourself unemployed. What's more, if you've chosen to sell products in a niche you're interested in, then you'll be able to do all this while essentially enjoying learning about a subject you love. And as you build a big audience, you'll find it's highly rewarding becoming an 'authority' in that area and having fan mail and a huge captive audience.

Keep it up and eventually you can start earning millions while you sleep.

Just make sure that this isn't your initial goal. Initially, your goal should be to earn some nice extra income.

This might sound trivial but it really isn't. Starting out with the right expectations and intentions will be the difference between giving up and enjoying a great career that can eventually set you free.

That is the first and most important 'secret' to affiliate marketing. But the rest are going to help you accelerate your progress with growth hacks and other techniques. This way, you won't have to wait all that long to start making the progress you deserve and that likely attracted you to affiliate marketing in the first place.

Chapter 2: How Affiliate Marketing Actually Works – The Mechanics

We've seen how affiliate marketing works but what we haven't addressed yet is the precise mechanics and how understanding this can help you to be more successful.

What happens for example, when someone clicks on one of your affiliate links?

The answer is 'cookies'. Cookies are small files that get saved on the computer and are handled by your browser. Websites can store cookies and then look for them and use them to keep you logged into Facebook, or to show you relevant adverts based on your browsing history.

When a buyer clicks on your link, they get sent to the checkout page for a specific product. At the same time though, a cookie will be stored on their computer which will identify them as having been referred by you. This means that when they make a purchase, the profits can be allocated to you.

Understanding this is important because it introduces a potential risk – that people will see what you're selling and navigate there of their own accord. This is called 'link bypassing' and it's worth your while to prevent this using link cloaking. That means using a redirect that sends people to your affiliate link while hiding the URL from them. You can do this using a simple bit of code:

```
<meta http-quiv="refresh" content="0;
url=http://www.example.com/affiliatelink">
```
Alternatively, you can use something like TinuUrl or Bit.ly.

It's also worth doing a little research into the affiliate program that you'll be working with. That's because the creator of a cookie also gets to set the lifespan. A cookie can last a few minutes, 90 days (most common) or it can last until the user actively chooses to delete their cookies/changes computer.

Of course it's much better for you to have an affiliate program with cookies that don't expire at all. Amazon has a 'session limited' cookie scheme for instance that only lasts 24 hours. That's actually pretty good in this case though, considering that people already know about Amazon and you can make money from other things people buy from the site that day.

What's also key to note is whether a subsequent affiliate can 'override' your cookie. This becomes relevant if someone should click your affiliate link, not make a purchase, then click someone else's affiliate link and buy. Who gets the money? This depends on whether the affiliate honors the first click or last click. If you are a 'lifetime referrer' then you will always be given credit for the referral regardless of what else happens subsequently.

Types of Affiliate Program and Choosing the Best Product

With those technical details out the way, it's time to start choosing affiliate products and programs. The first step is deciding which type of affiliate program you want to join. Do you want to sell a digital product? A physical product? Or a service?

The best answer for most beginners will be a digital product. This means something like an eBook, a free report or a digital course. There's no cost associated with production, storage or delivery here and as such the product creator gets a much bigger slice of the profit. What's more, they have more profit to share with you and that means you can earn up to 50-75% from each sale.

To find these products, you should look at an affiliate network such as JVZoo, ClickBank, Commission Junction or Warrior Special Offers.

To use one of these sites, all you need to do is sign up, browse through the available products and then apply to work as an affiliate for a few. You can see data and information about each one, such as the number of sales, the cost etc.

From there, you want to choose a digital product that is making a lot of sales but also offers you a good amount of cash per sale. Think too about how you're going to market each of those products and what 'angle' you'll go with to make it attractive to your audience.

Trying out the product is a very good idea, as is finding one that offers free marketing materials that the product creator designed. Some will come with free landing pages, blog posts, email autoresponder sequences and more that you can utilize for free.

Promoting digital products means you make more money per sale and it means there's less that can go wrong. It's also the preferred method by many digital marketers, which means you'll find a lot more advice and help.

Some people though will feel more comfortable selling physical products which they can do by signing up to Amazon Associates or Shareasale. People like selling physical products because they have a much wider audience. It's a certain type of person who is willing to spend $50 on an eBook; anyone who is a technophobe, who wants something physical, or who is savvy enough to know they can get most information for free will not be interested.

On the other hand, we all spend money on physical items – from Grandmas, to jocks to genius coders. This means you have a much larger potential audience. Unfortunately though, physical products also cost a lot more to produce and to ship and normally they go through more channels before you get the opportunity to promote them. When you sell a product through Amazon for instance, the money is going to get split between you, the product creator, Amazon, the delivery company and possibly even another reseller.

As such, affiliates on Amazon tend to get as much as 4-8% per sale as opposed to 50-75%. The products will also often be cheaper and less geared towards getting digital sales. Why would someone click your link to buy a computer when they can just go to their local technology store? These are the considerations you'll need to take into account when you start trying to sell physical products rather than digital ones. Of course, there's nothing to stop you from selling both types of product, though then you do risk cannibalizing some of your own sales.

Ultimately, it makes a lot more sense to start with digital products because you can make a bigger commission from fewer sales. When you're not yet getting the sheer volume of visitors you need to make hundreds of sales, selling digital products is still the quickest route to making more money.

Finally, you can look at selling services or memberships. These will often provide you with what are known as 'lifetime commissions'. For instance, if you can get people to sign up to a gambling site, you might be able to earn commission from them for the lifetime of their membership. Get enough of these and you can be set for life – but of course, there are unique challenges here too.

There are far fewer of these sorts of affiliate schemes for instance (for obvious reasons) and normally the best way to find them is to visit the sites in person. This means you can end up with lots of separate accounts and in turn, things can get a little cumbersome. This is more complex and perhaps not a great starting point for complete beginners.

A Few More Tips for Choosing Your Affiliate Product

Something else to consider when choosing an affiliate product, is whether it's something you will be able to sell. Not only must it be possible to sell generally, but you also need to be able to sell it personally. That means that ideally, it should be on a topic that you find interesting and that you something about.

When creating a blog or building a mailing list, you will usually need to write a lot of blog posts and e-mails on the topic of the product in order to build trust, provide value and offer a reason for people to come to your website in the first place. If you aren't careful and you choose a subject you know nothing about, you'll quickly find this tiring and boring and you'll be more likely to quit. What's more, is that readers might be able to tell that you aren't in fact an expert on the subject and this will undermine the points you make and lose your readers' trust in your information.

At the same time, you also need to think about the advantages that are unique to you, such as any routes to market you might have. A route to market is any direct link you have with a potential audience – such as a blog or a magazine. If you already have a blog, then of course you need to choose a product that your readers will find interesting.

But you might also have some additional routes to market. For instance, think about your contacts: do you have the e-mail address of any top bloggers? Are you friends with the editor of an industry magazine?

In other words, it basically boils down to choosing a product that you already know you can sell. Even if you don't have a direct route to market, think about what the best routes to market for each product might be and how you could go about reaching them. Don't choose a product then think about how you'll sell it – choose the product because you know you can sell it. We'll be talking more about this later.

Big Niche, Little Niche

Another consideration is whether to pick a 'big niche' or a 'little niche'. Of course, every internet marketer knows that your 'niche' is your industry which at the same time will dictate your subject matter.

So if you're selling an eBook on getting abs, your niche and your industry are 'fitness'. On the other hand, if you're selling an eBook on making money online, then your niche is online business.

Making money online is actually the biggest niche you'll find when it comes to digital products with affiliate schemes. In fact, WSOPro (Warrior Forum Special Offers) is entirely dedicated to digital marketing products. Just behind digital marketing as a niche are the fitness niche and the online dating niche.

This is a good thing because these are proven niches. People are happy to spend money to make money and they'll also spend money to look and feel better or to find love. These are also subjects that appeal to everyone. So if you're looking for a product with a proven track record, it will likely be in these areas.

But there's also a problem here: these areas are highly competitive and can be oversaturated for the same reasons. If you want to reach this audience then you're going to need to spend more money on PPC advertising as you'll be bidding against more competitors. Likewise, if you want to create a blog, you'll be competing with a much larger number of other blogs for the top spot on Google and for readers.

Conversely if you create a blog on 'Super Meat Boy' then

you'll be among maybe two other fan sites and you'll find that you can very quickly get seen by pretty much your entire audience. Likewise, you'll probably be able to pay to advertise on Google or Facebook for these terms without spending much money.

The same goes for writing about a specific job or profession. If you're selling an eBook on 'stage lighting techniques' then you'll find it much easier to reach those professionals without spending vast amounts of money.

But at the same time, the products will also appeal to a much smaller market. This means that it won't take as long to saturate the market and you likely won't make as many sales over the long term. The answer? Often the best strategy will be to start smaller and then to build your way up to reach the bigger niches.

Another option is to choose an affiliate product that aims at a smaller cross section of a much larger niche. For instance, 'fitness for the over 50s' is a much smaller chunk of the larger 'fitness' niche. The same goes for 'digital marketing for students'.

One more consideration though is who that target demographic is and specifically how much disposable income they have. In this regard, aiming at the over fifty makes more sense than aiming for students!

Why do Product Creators on Digital Affiliate Networks Give Away So Much Profit?

Something you might be asking yourself at this point is why a digital product manufacturer would be willing to give away 75% of their profits; what's in it for them?

To understand this, it's worth considering the power of scaling up. Sure, they're only making 25% per sale but if they have 20 affiliates selling 100 copies of their item a day, they're still going to make far more than any of those individual affiliates. More importantly, they'll probably be able to earn much more than they would selling the product on their own.

The more commission the affiliate promoter offers, the more people will come on board (versus other products) and that means they'll be able to continually scale up their profits. Additionally, they're probably still making money from their own marketing activities where they'll be making 100% per sale. The sales they get from you are on top of their natural earnings.

Your Beginner Strategy: Don't Reinvent the Wheel

The great thing about affiliate marketing through JVZoo or ClickBank is that you can start earning nearly as much as the product creator themselves without having to create anything. There's really very little reason to spend lots of time and money creating a product when you could just find one ready-made and earn the same amount of money for you right away.

But saving time and money is only one big benefit of affiliate marketing. The other is the fact that the products you'll be selling will come 'pre validated'.

What this basically means, is that you know for sure that there's demand out there for the product you're selling and that people actually want to buy it.

Conversely, when you create a product of your own, there's a chance that after putting all the time and effort in to build it, you'll find that no one actually wants it. In that case, all the marketing prowess in the world won't help you and you'll actually come out worse off than you started.

With affiliate marketing, you get to choose a product that is already selling lots of units and in some cases you can use their exact sales scripts in order to sell it. This is a proven quantity and as such, there's little that can go wrong.

This is literally a 'cut and paste' business and all that's left to you is to find your own audience.

Unfortunately, many affiliate marketers don't realize this and they want to get clever with creating their own unique business strategy. The same goes for all the people who try inventing their own new app, or becoming the next massive blogger. That's all well and good but 9 times out of 10, they will fail. If you're really serious about earning money, you don't need to re-invent the wheel. Just find what you know works and use that exact business model to earn money yourself.

This is the smartest way to start making lots of money as an affiliate. Find what works and then go with it – don't try and be clever. Once you've had some initial success and earned some cash then you can look at creating your own product or changing the world. For now, settle for earning money in a tried and tested manner, quickly and efficiently.

Scaling Up

Once you find the right product and you begin making some money from it, you can continue with this 'repeat what works' strategy in a very simple manner: by repeating it!

In other words, if you are making money from a certain

digital product in a certain niche, then why not just completely mimic that model and start selling two different digital products? That quickly, you can double your income as well as giving yourself a backup and a more secure model as a result.

Alternatively, you can just start spending more on your PPC ad campaign to drive more traffic. Build mini business models and monitor your conversion rate and then, only once you've proven that they make ROI, start spending more money on them to multiply your earnings.

Chapter 3: Time to Make Sales

As mentioned, there will be some cases where you can find digital products that are selling very well and that actually provide you with their sales page and even the e-mails they use. If you can find such a product then go for it, especially if they share their conversion rate. This removes variables from your process thereby allowing you to fine tune your business model all the more quickly.

But not all digital products will provide these materials meaning that you'll need to create your own sales page and email sequence. Likewise, there will be times when you see ways to improve the sales page you've received.

That's where this section comes in: making things sell. By the end, you should know how to take your conversions from a measly 1% and boost them to a highly profitable 10%.

What is a Sales Page? Creating the Layout

The first question is: what is a sales page? A sales page is an entire page on a website that is completely dedicated to selling one product. This means there will be no external links to other pages and no other products being promoted. The entire page is designed to draw people to the 'buy now' button and to convince them why they should in fact buy.

Chances are that you have visited sales pages in the past and you'll recognize them through their design. These pages are generally very vertical and have a very thin passage of text that encourages lots of scrolling. This is no accident – the act of scrolling down the page makes visitors feel as though they're becoming more 'committed' to the product and the further they scroll, the less they will normally want to then come away empty handed – it feels like a waste.

Meanwhile there will be no navigation or links to other pages – for precisely the reason that these distract the reader away from the 'buy now' option. Finally, these pages are often designed to be either bright red or orange around the edges. There's a reason for this too: red and orange are colors that actually cause the heartrate to increase and make us feel uncomfortable. These colors make us want to act quickly to leave or to buy which makes us more impulsive.

If you think of fast food stores, then you'll find that often these are red or orange in terms of their interior design often too. The reason in this case is similar – they want to increase turnover and get people out of the store more quickly so they can serve more customers and make more money!

Finally, there's one more key thing to consider when creating your landing page and that is trust and barriers to sale.

When someone lands on your website and sees you are selling a product, they will very often be suspicious of you to begin with and concerned that it could be a scam. People still don't like handing over their details online so, if they think your sales page looks dodgy, they'll often just leave. Your job is to make it as simple for them to buy as possible and to make them trust in the system you've set up to enable that.

This is one of the big advantages to selling products via Amazon Associates – here, your checkout page is Amazon itself which instills buyer trust. Most likely they already use Amazon so they might even be able to use the 'buy with one click' option to save themselves time and to really encourage those impulsive buying decisions.

If you use JVZoo or Clickbank, then the sales page will be built by those sites and this will likely be a factor to consider when you choose which network to go with. Is their checkout page professional looking? Would you be happy to spend your money through it?

The initial impression you make on your visitors will be the landing page itself; so it's worth making sure you put the time and effort into creating something that looks professional and trustworthy. One of the easiest and best ways to do this is to use a tool like Optimize Press. Optimize Press is a WordPress theme which you can install with a single click to make your WordPress site into a traditional sales page. When you do this, you'll be using ready-made layouts and images that have been optimized over thousands of sites and that are constantly being refined. Then all you have to do is to enter the text.

Remember what we said about not reinventing the wheel? Why make it more difficult for yourself when you already have the means to create something professional and proven.
Otherwise, consider using a third party developer that has a good track record. This is better than attempting to design the sales page yourself and coming up with something that looks less than perfectly professional.

Writing Your Sales Script

In fact, a convincing sales page is all about your sales script. The text you use to sell your product is going to be the single biggest determining factor when it comes to your conversion rates and this is something that is worth taking the time to learn.

There's a lot to this though, so bear with me while I explain the ins and outs of good persuasive writing.

Grabbing Attention

The first, and biggest, challenge when it comes to making sales will be to grab the attention of your visitors, to communicate that there's something here worth reading and that they shouldn't navigate away from the site.

The unfortunate reality is that most people are in a rush all the time, have lots of work to do and don't have time to read through large amounts of text. That means you can't expect your audience to stick around unless you give them a very good reason. You need to grab them with a hook right away and then reel them in.

One of the best ways to do this is to give your sales page a narrative structure. This means you need to turn your pitch into a story that your audience can relate to. The reason this is so effective is that we always want to know how stories end. Have you ever started watching a trashy program late at night that you don't care about, only to find yourself unable to look away until the very end? In such scenarios you'll often watch for hours even though you aren't enjoying it! This is the power of narrative and it's a very human impulse that you can use to your advantage.

Another advantage of using a narrative is that it makes the situation more relatable. By telling people that you used to be in the same position as them, you can get them interested and at the same time you'll be much more convincing.

This in fact is the basic structure of many a successful sales page: introduce a problem and then offer a solution. If you're selling a book on abs, then the 'problem' is a lack of fitness or inability to lose weight. The solution of course is your eBook and you're going to frame all this in a first person narrative where you discuss how you were once overweight until you found this incredible strategy that they can read about in your eBook.

Obesity, tiredness and sluggishness are one type of 'problem'. This is an emotional and abstract problem that you can make anyone to relate to.

The other type of problem is something specific and simple. For instance, if you are selling a book on stage lighting you would look for a very specific and simple problem in this niche. Perhaps people struggle to afford the stage lighting equipment they need. Maybe the lights keep falling over… I'm not an expert in this field and that's why it's not a niche I would choose (remember we discussed picking a field you were familiar with?).

Anyway, the point is that selling a product that answers a very specific need is always a good strategy as it simplifies your job of finding people who have that problem. This should come into play when you pick your product: find a product that solves a clear and easily defined problem.

Other things that grab attention are bold statements and rhetorical questions. Rhetorical questions work well because they force the reader to think and reflect. This means they can't just glance over the text and not take it in, but now have to actually engage with it and think about what it means for them.

Bold statements grab attention simply through their brazenness. This could mean that you open up with an unbelievable figure, or with a controversial claim. You can later explain yourself but initially this is a great way to get people to stop what they're doing and to read.

Flow and Break Points

Just as you need to quickly grab attention, you also need to make sure that you hold it and don't let go – even for a second.

This is where flow comes in and it's very important to make sure that your text flows smoothly and without obvious breaks. The text should be so compelling that it pulls the reader from one line to the next without giving them the time to think about leaving.

This is another reason for the long narrow design that so many sales pages use – it naturally encourages flow.

The same is true with short sentences and lots of space. Ideally you want to make your content as 'skim friendly as possible', especially considering that most web users skim and don't read. You do this by spacing out your text but also by using lots of headers. In fact, it's generally considered good practice to write your headers so that the entire narrative of the text can be discerned simply by reading the headings.

This is also a reason that sales pages will often underline and bold sections. A massive, dense block of text will always be off putting and hard to read for someone in a hurry. On the other hand though…
Imagine a text that spaces out its sentences…

That uses lots of bold statements…

And that engages the user with a strong narrative.

And rhetorical questions.

How much more effective might that be?

See the difference?

Another consideration when it comes to flow is maintaining the interest of your audience and ensuring that your content is never dull or boring. If you start repeating yourself, or if the quality of your writing drops, you can lose your readers. A good solution here is to read the text through yourself and get other people to and then identify the points where you occasionally lose interest. Once you do, just fix that section by spacing it out more or using more interesting language.

Finally, you can also make sure you hold attention by directly addressing any concerns the reader may have. The big problem you're contending with here is people saying 'yeah, but'. If they have heard your pitch before they'll be cynical and they won't engage with what you're saying. That's why it's your job to anticipate the problems they'll have and then answer them before they become an issue.

That's why you'll often encounter the 'I know what you're thinking' line:

'I know what you're thinking – this is just another training program that you'll never complete! You've tried countless just like it right? What makes this one any different? I had the same exact thought but see, that's where Brutal Ab Training is so effective. Because it works so quickly and because it's such a fun challenge, it incredibly easy to stick to!'

Appealing to Authority and Statistics

The above paragraph would be very effective at convincing people that your product isn't just like every other. But if you want to take it one step further, you can also reference statistics or authority figures. While we all know that statistics are remarkably easy to manipulate, this doesn't at all prevent them from being very effective tools for persuasion.

Follow that last statement up with a statistic and you make it much more believable and convincing. For instance:

'Because it works so quickly and because it's such a fun challenge, it incredibly easy to stick to! Maybe that's why the program has a success rate of 95% across over 3,000 users!'

Equally effective would be to quote an authority in your field as this can similarly lend weight and credence to your statements. Even just quoting a user can be effective – especially as social influence plays such a big role in decision making. If you have quotes from a bunch of people singing the praises of your program, it not only makes the program sound effective, it also makes it sound like something that's new and exciting, that 'everyone is trying'. In turn, that increases the desirability associated with it.

Value Proposition

Most important of all though, when it comes to your sales page is to keep in mind your value proposition. A value proposition is essentially the thing that you are promising to do for your buyer via the product. This is what gives the product its value.

This should be at the forefront of your sales pitch because it is what will give the product you are selling an emotional hook – and most things we buy are based on emotion rather than logic.
The old saying goes that you don't sell a hat, you sell a warm head. It's much easier to sell a warm head because a cold head is a problem – and a warm head is something that will make people happier and make them more confortable.

Likewise, if you're selling an eBook on fitness you aren't selling a book. Instead, you're selling fitness, you're selling confidence and you're selling a better love life – these are all the valuable things that having abs provide you with. Selling a book on making money online? Then you're really selling financial freedom and freedom from debt or money problems. You can charge a lot more for great abs and a great love life than you can for a PDF!

This is incredibly important as it is ultimately what is going to get your readers to really want your products rather than just being interested. This creates the emotion that will lead to the snap decision to buy – as long as you've made your sales page look professional and you've provided lots of opportunities for people to click your CTA button (Call To Action button).

Creating Urgency

When you get people reading your sales page, you're really trying to stir up a nice little 'neurochemical cocktail' in their brain. You want to get them to focus with your bold statements, your narrative structure and the problem you've outlined that needs to be solved.

You've then focused on the value proposition and you've got them imagining what life would be like with those abs, or all that money. This then creates a real sense of desire and makes the reader feel as though they must have the item that you're promoting.

Now, you're going to create anxiety. The anxiety comes from the thought that the product won't be around forever and that it's going to disappear/go up in price. You actually have no control over whether that's true as an affiliate but that doesn't mean your sales page can't vaguely allude to the idea that the product won't be in stock forever, or that the price will likely go up in the near future.

This creates 'urgency' and that in turn prevents the user from wanting to leave the site and 'think about it'. You need to make sure they act now rather than later. You can do this by offering a limited time discount (some affiliate schemes give you flexibility over the pricing), or by saying there's only limited stock and thereby creating scarcity (this also makes the product seem more popular).

Now you'll get that knee jerk sale you're looking for.

Removing Risk

Finally, you should try to remove any risk associated with buying the product. This is important because human beings are naturally 'risk averse'. This means that we are more motivated by avoiding a loss than we are by achieving gain. So if you let someone play a game where they had a 75% chance of earning $100 and a 25% chance of losing $20, they may still not play.

When we're buying, this comes into play if we think the product might be low quality or if we think that it could be a scam. This is why you should always offer a '100% money back guarantee'. Better yet, consider offering a 'try before you buy'. All the big affiliate networks offer the former while there may be ways you can provide the latter (giving away the first chapter, after checking with the product creator). Either way, this will help you remove any reason that the reader has not to buy.

Chapter 4: Platforms You Can Use to Make Sales

Of course your sales page is only one place where you can promote and sell affiliate products. Another place for instance, is within the body of your articles, which will be a more passive approach.

Blog Posts

If you're running a blog and using this to create a big audience that you can drive to your sales page, you can also use those blog posts to make sales. All you have to do is to embed your sales page URLs within the body of those posts.

You might just mention how 'X product' is really good for whatever you're writing about and then leave the link there for a reader to click. If they're really interested in your content and you're doing a great job of demonstrating your knowledge and making it exciting, this can lead to a few extra clicks.

This is an especially good strategy to use when selling physical products as an Amazon affiliate and you can leverage the reader's curiosity.

For instance, you might write an article on dating and mention how some people will even use pheromones or oxytocin sprays to make themselves more appealing (and here's a great product to check out). Clearly, this is something people might click on just out of curiosity even if they don't intend to buy. But because Amazon has a 24 hour cookie, you can then make commissions on anything that they might subsequently decide to buy on the site – even if they come back later of their own accord!

Likewise, you can use links to physical products in blog posts and then actively sell them. A lot of bloggers make their primary income from reviewing Amazon products and linking to them. Many people will read reviews of laptops for instance before they buy and if they follow your link after reading your comments, this can result in a big chunk of cash!

Email Marketing

Something else that lends itself very nicely to affiliate marketing is email marketing. Simply build a large mailing list from your blog and then pitch products to them.

Of course you'll need to create a compelling blog and give your readers a good reason to subscribe in order to build this list. Once you've done that though, you'll then have direct access to a huge audience of people who trust you and who actively gave you permission to contact them.

You can now send out your sales copy over the course of several emails. While also providing value via tips, entertainment or general information, you can begin building interest and anticipation for a product. The great thing about this is that your audience will have to wait before you send them the call to action to know how to buy. People always want what they can't have, so if you do this well then you can build excitement for a product to fever pitch before making your move.

Affiliate Marketing in Person

Believe it or not, you can even use affiliate marketing in person. Alternatively, you can do it by posting flyers just as you might if you were selling a product or service on commission as an employee.

Here you just need a simple URL that people can type into their browser. This could be achieved using link cloaking or using a sales page of your own creation. You can add the link to the flier and hand it out to people in the street, post it through people's doors. You can even do a pitch in person to explain why the product is so good.

This is a strategy that works particularly well for lifetime membership programs. For instance, if you can find a bingo site with an affiliate program, print off some fliers, and then hand them out in an area with a large elderly population, you can quickly get some people to sign up who will earn you an income for the entire time they are members.

Notice how different strategies work better for different types of affiliate product and for different demographics? Once again, the key here is to have synergy between your product selection, your own blog and your routes to market. Think of everything before committing to your chosen first product!

Using Your Existing Routes to Market

As mentioned, there's a good chance that whoever you are, you will have at least one good route to market – often it's just a matter of thinking hard enough.

For instance, it might be that among your friends, you know someone who runs a magazine on gardening with a readership of 5,000. This is a fantastically easy route to market for you, especially as there's probably a website with a forum involved too. Just ask nicely and see if they will cover your story.

Another example might be your old college paper. If you're alumni from a university with a particularly big fashion department, then this could be the perfect place to sell your eBook on 'getting into the fashion industry'.

Essentially this is a form of influencer marketing, with the only difference being that you're aiming for an influencer you already know versus trying desperately to find one.

Influencer Marketing - Plan B?

Try diligently to find one!

Another great way to accomplish the same thing as the above is simply to find an influencer that you can work with and reach out to them. You can either pay them to give you a shout-out or you can do something in return as a favor.

One example is to write a guest post for a blog. This is a strategy commonly used to build links to a website, but it can actually be just as effective when used as a way to get direct sales. Find a blog that accepts contributions from other writers, then offer to write them an article for free that they can publish on their site, in exchange for including a link to your website (which is just a landing page with your affiliate product). If you can get on a blog with hundreds of thousands of people reading, then you can potentially get your link seen by thousands overnight which could be just enough to set you up for life! Yes, sometimes it really does come down to that one link on that one key site.

How do you reach these big influencers who are leading your niche?

There are two strategies that actually work:

a) Interact with them in person – Go to networking events or even hire their services. Either way, develop an actual relationship in person.

b) Build your way up – Don't approach Tony Robbins when you have a readership of one. Instead, aim for someone much smaller and then gradually look for bigger and bigger affiliates. This way you should always be 'on a level' with the person you're asking for help which means there's more likely to be something in it for them as well as you. It also means you're less likely to get laughed out of their inbox…

Chapter 5: Content Marketing - Marketing Your Email List, Blogs and Sales Page

The above strategies are what are known in the industry as 'growth hacks'. That is to say that they're techniques you can use to quickly increase your exposure to a much wider audience, rather than to grow slowly using the normal trajectory.

More often, though, you'll find yourself taking a more straightforward approach by gradually rising through the ranks via SEO (search engine optimization), social media and content marketing.

The Power of Content Marketing

The key here is the content marketing. Content marketing simply means creating lots of value on your website by writing high quality blog posts, articles and features.

The objective here is to give people a reason to visit your site – and content is the main reason we visit any website on the net. At the same time though, your content is what's going to demonstrate your knowledge and know-how. You can use this to build trust and authority so that any products you recommend will be more likely to be taken seriously by your audience.

This will encourage people to sign up to your mailing list and will make affiliates want to work with you. Generally, this is what will help you to go from 0 viewers a day to 10,000 viewers a day. Make sure that your content is long enough to offer real value (around 1,800 words according to research) and that it is unique and engaging. You can't write articles that are derivative and old hat and expect people to rush to subscribe to your mailing list!

Another tip is to make sure that you are putting in the time and effort to create as much content as possible. *This is an area where quantity counts almost as much as quality!* The key here is that in order to make a full time living from a blog, you need to treat it like a full time job in terms of the work you put in.

Be on every social media site as well and make sure that you provide value on here as well so that you give people an actual reason to follow you.Do this consistently and you'll gradually build an audience that trusts you and that you can sell to time and time again.

PPC Pay-Per-Click

In terms of PPC (pay per click) advertising, there are two main networks you will likely choose from. These are Google AdWords and Facebook Ads. The former lets you place your adverts alongside specific key word searches right on the SERPs ('Search Engine Results Pages'), the latter allows you to show ads on users' home feeds.

The great thing about both these types of advertising, other than their pay per click nature, is the fact that they let you carefully target a very specific type of visitor. Since you pay for each click, your objective is not to get as many people as possible to go to your website but rather to make sure that only the people most likely to buy from you see the ads and click on them.

On Google AdWords, you accomplish this by targeting phrases that only your potential buyers would search for. So if you're selling a book on getting abs, you might target phrases like 'how to get great abs' but use Google's 'negative keywords' tool to filter anyone who uses the term 'free' (seeing as they're not looking to buy anything). You would then put the price of your eBook right in the description alongside your ad so that only people who are likely to buy from you will consider clicking it – thereby improving your ROI.

On Facebook you can do something similar by targeting your readers based on their age, their sex, their location, their job, their hobbies etc. This means that if you're selling an eBook on wedding planning, you can target specifically women who are engaged. Again, this greatly reduces the number of people who will click your ads who won't be a potentially relevant customer.

Once more, your key to success is to think of all this when you choose your product. Ask yourself: how easily can you target your visitors?

Chapter 6 – Conclusions

So there you have it: everything you need to know to be much more effective at affiliate marketing than about 90% of people who get into it.

We've covered a lot of information and a ton of secrets but all in a rather quick manner. To finish then, let's highlight just a few of the biggest and most important tips that we've gone over:

Affiliate Marketing Takes Time

To be successful at affiliate marketing you need to approach it with the right expectations and plan. To start with, aim to earn some money on the side. Don't think you'll be a millionaire overnight – but that's okay. Aim to supplement your income doing something you love and in time you'll start making your riches.

Copy and Paste Your Business

Don't reinvent the wheel – keep it simple as much as possible. Choose a digital product that has lots of proven sales and use the exact business model as far as possible to benefit from that proven success.

To scale, just rinse and repeat.

Start Small and Climb the Ranks

If you don't have lots of money to invest in PPC, then aim for a smaller niche to begin with. If you can find an affiliate product aimed at a particular industry that solves a specific problem for example, this will often be a great place to start.

Then you can reinvest the money you make here once you've saturated that smaller market.

Think About How You'll Market Before You Choose Your Product

Don't pick a product and then worry about how to reach an audience. Instead, pick a product with an idea of how you're going to sell it.

What is the value proposition?

What routes to market do you already have?

How easy is it to target the specific   demographic?

Use these strategies, be consistent and you will find that affiliate marketing really can make you rich and allow you to earn an entirely passive income. Stick with it, enjoy it and it will happen!

For more online marketing and business training including detailed growth opportunities go to www.IQPress.org

ABOUT THE AUTHOR

IQ Press, Inc. is a small publishing company dedicated to providing access to educational materials primarily in small business start-up and development. Their mission is to bring the reader useful information that can be implemented with a small capital outlay and generate income streams for the reader to implement.

We hope you enjoy these reports and that they will help improve your life.

To get a jumpstart in online marketing download our exclusive quick start guide here: www.IQPress.org/Quickstart

Check out more great reports at:

www.IQPress.org

REFERENCE MATERIALS

Other books you may enjoy to help you on your journey:

Affiliate Marketing Secrets: You did become an affiliate marketer to become rich, right? OK, so now what? Start here and learn how to take your fledgling affiliate marketing company to the next step. This report is packed with secret tips and tricks to help you grow your company quickly. After all, your goal is to add customers and new products quickly and expand your business without taking on more risk.

In this short read you will find dozens of ideas to help move your company forward. Not a bunch of theoretical ideas but actual tested tips and techniques to move you towards your goal quickly.

Finding the Best Affiliate Products to Promote: How do I find the best products to sell? Now that you know about affiliate marketing and its great income potential, how can you choose what product(s) to promote? You want one with high demand but not too much competition. You need to choose the category, the product, the venue, the program, etc... That's quite a lot for a new company owner! We can help. This guide will walk you through all these decisions and keep you from getting in a bad place with a product that has poor sell-through.

Affiliate Marketing and Success Systems: This report is a compendium of tips and ideas to help keep you on track with your affiliate marketing business. You want an automatic money machine? We'll show you not only how to grow but also to get that growth on autopilot! With a few simple programs you can get the company to generate a continuous income stream. That's why you went into this type business, right?

Using this report will turbocharge your results and help you simply and effectively grow your sales. Bring in a constant stream of new customers and new products to offer your existing customers for a generous income. You could even quit your job if you wanted! Imagine all that free time while still enjoying a great income.

Available exclusively at: www.IQPress.org